presented to: _____

from: _____

THE
Twenty-Third Psalm

for
Caregivers

With love and gratitude
to the Shepherd of my soul.
—*Carmen Leal*

Contents

It is a kingly task, believe me, to help the afflicted.
—Ovid

THE
TWENTY-THIRD
Psalm

-for.-
Caregivers

CARMEN LEAL

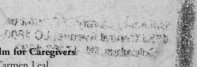

Published by AMG Publishers
6815 Shallowford Rd.
Chattanooga, Tennessee 37421

ISBN 0-89957-136-0

First printing—June 2004

Cover designed by Market Street Design, Inc., Chattanooga, Tennessee
Interior design and typesetting by The Livingstone Corporation, Carol Stream, Illinois.
Edited and proofread by Tammy Campbell, Dan Penwell, The Livingstone
Corporation, and Warren Baker.

Printed in Italy
10 09 08 07 06 05 04 –L– 8 7 6 5 4 3 2 1

Introduction

"For I know the plans I have for you," declares the LORD, "plans to prosper you and not to harm you, plans to give you hope and a future." —Jeremiah 29:11

THAT'S ALL I NEED TO KNOW

A teacher assigned Psalm 23 as the Sunday school memory verse. Because it was long, the teacher gave the children two weeks before they were to stand before peers and parents to recite the passage.

The world doesn't care what you know until they know that you care.
—David Harvard

One by one the children, some skipping, others dragging their feet, made their way to the front of the class and began reciting the familiar words. A little girl with an obviously new dress and shiny shoes took the first turn and flawlessly shared the well-known scripture. A towhead reluctantly came forward and, to his parents' obvious surprise, made it to the end with fewer than expected mistakes.

The parade continued, with recitations ranging from the serious to the humorous until the final child took to the stage. He was excited about the task but he just couldn't remember what he had practiced over and over. He looked at his mother who was mouthing the words. It didn't help. He managed to recite the first line but couldn't remember anything else. The other children giggled at his hesitation. That made things even worse.

Just as the teacher stepped forward to rescue the little boy, he tried one more time. He stood tall, took a deep breath, and with an infectious grin said, "The Lord is my shepherd . . . and that's all I need to know!"

The shepherd's psalm is one of the most familiar passages of the Bible. Books have been written and sermons preached about these words penned by David. We've heard it prayed amidst tears and plaintive cries at graveside services in both real life and the movies. The words have been set to music, used as greeting card verses, and framed with stunning artwork.

But what does this familiar psalm say to caregivers?

Some of you are like the little boy who couldn't remember all the words. He did, however, remember the most important words. Hopefully, you do, too. *The Lord is your shepherd and that's all you need to know.* Somehow, in the midst of loss and obligations is the knowledge that He not only gets you through each day as a caregiver, but He is your personal shepherd in every area of your life.

There are those of you who might have memorized Psalm 23 as a child but have since forgotten the all-important first line—*The LORD is my Shepherd*. The drudgery of caregiving is a reality to you, but the fact that the Lord is *your* Shepherd may not be real to you.

Whether you have planted every word of that psalm in your heart . . . are filled with doubt that those words were written for you . . . or are somewhere in between, this is truly the caregiver's psalm. A caregiver's job often seems thankless as we bathe, feed, comfort, fight battles, cut through red tape, and give direction. I'm sure our heavenly Father, our Caregiver, often feels His job is thankless as He cares for us. Thankfully, He continues to care for, love, and guide us, even when we are as stupid and stubborn as sheep.

Pastor Orlando Rivera, former pastor of Northland, A Church Distributed in Longwood, Florida, said, "When God wants to woo us and make Himself known to us in the most intimate way possible, He gives us stories. Stories to capture our fancy. Stories that make us laugh and cry. Stories that make His presence deep and rich in our souls. Yes, when God wants to make our character into His own, He gives us stories."

God wants to make our character His own. The stories, scriptures, hymns, and quotes in each following chapter seek to comfort and teach as He embraces us as our Caring Shepherd.

Yes, the Lord is our shepherd and that might be all we need to know. But inside this most beloved of all psalms, there lays wisdom and comfort. No matter your past or your future, hold on to the fact that the Lord is *your* shepherd.

The Lord is my shepherd,
I shall not be in want.
He makes me lie down in green pastures,
He leads me beside quiet waters,
He restores my soul.
He guides me in paths of righteousness for his name's sake.
Even though I walk through the valley of the shadow of death,
I will fear no evil, for you are with me;
your rod and your staff, they comfort me.
You prepare a table before me in the presence of my enemies.
You anoint my head with oil; my cup overflows.
Surely goodness and love will follow me all the days of my life,
and I will dwell in the house of the LORD forever.

CHAPTER ONE

THE SHEPHERD WHO *Cares*

"THE LORD IS MY SHEPHERD"

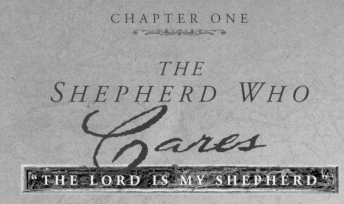

IN AS CLEAR A VOICE AS POSSIBLE

My husband David, because of a terminal neurological disease, was having increasing difficulty feeding himself; he could swallow only with a great deal of effort. As I fed him one day, with more food landing on his shirt than in his mouth, David and I went through the usual "change the shirt" game.

"David, lift up your arms," I pleaded. "If you do, we can go get some ice cream."

David's garbled speech made his response to my urging impossible to comprehend. However, I did figure out that

Know that the LORD is God. It is he who made us, and we are his; we are his people, the sheep of his pasture.

—Psalm 100:3

he had no intention of lifting his arms or cooperating as I changed the shirt.

I felt myself tense up, and I sighed in frustration. I didn't need this. Try as I would, I simply couldn't understand what he was saying, and we weren't moving any nearer to our goal—a clean shirt.

"David, my job is to feed you, make sure you take your medications, and help the doctors and nurses. Your job is to help me to help you. You need to lift your arms, please."

With an endearing smile so like that of the man I married before the ravages of his illness took over David said, "No. My job is to say 'I love you,' in as clear a voice as possible."

Isn't that how we are with our heavenly Caregiver? If you're anything like me, you say, "God, your job is to heal my loved one. Your job is to provide me with the money and support I need to be a caregiver. You need to make my job easier."

Fortunately, God knows His job better than we do. He patiently says, "No. My job is to say 'I love you,' in as clear a voice as possible."

C.S. Lewis wrote, "God whispers in our pleasures but shouts in our pain." Whether God is whispering or shouting, He tells us to, "Be still and know that I am God" (Ps 46:10).

When we are still, when our turbulent emotions become placid, then we can hear His voice as He tells us of His love. We can hear His voice when we get unexpected respite. A gentle smile from the one we are caring for is God's way of whispering His love. God can be heard in the lack of outside demands on a particularly stressful day, or when the insurance company actually pays their share without a fight.

Oswald Chambers's words speak even to God's silence: "You say, 'But He has not answered.' He has. He is so near to you that His silence is the answer. His silence is big with terrific meaning that you cannot understand yet, but presently you will."

In whispering, shouting, and yes, even in silence, our God, our Caregiver, is enunciating His love in as clear a voice as possible.

> *If you want to hear God's voice clearly and you are uncertain, then remain in His presence until He changes this uncertainty.*
> —Corrie ten Boom

I believe in the sun, even though it doesn't shine.
I believe in love, even when it isn't shown.
I believe in God, even when he doesn't speak.
—Written on the wall of a concentration camp by a prisoner.

He tends his flock like a shepherd: He gathers the lambs in his arms and carries
them close to his heart; He gently leads those that have young.
—Isaiah 40:11

LEANING ON THE EVERLASTING ARMS

—Elisha A. Hoffman

What a fellowship, what a joy divine,

Leaning on the everlasting arms;

What a blessedness, what a peace is mine,

Leaning on the everlasting arms.

CHAPTER TWO

THE
SHEPHERD WHO
Provides

"I SHALL NOT BE IN WANT"

TRUSTING GOD

In the middle of my caregiving journey, circumstances dictated a move five thousand miles from home. With no family or friends and dwindling resources, I felt ill-equipped to provide all that was needed for my husband and teenage sons. Because David was under retirement age, he didn't qualify for the many programs created to ease the burden for senior citizens. We had no

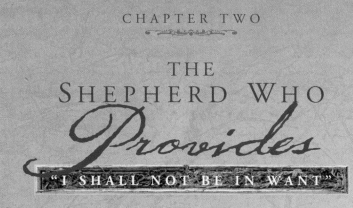

Therefore do not worry about tomorrow, for tomorrow will worry about itself. Each day has enough trouble of its own.
—Matthew 6:34

health insurance, so the increasingly large burden of medical bills, plus housing and all the other expenses needed for a family of four, fell on my head.

In my heart I knew I wasn't alone—I had God. I knew that He would provide all I needed, but it seemed that every waking hour involved cutting through bureaucratic red tape or trying to be everything to everyone. As the months turned into years, and the bills and isolation mounted, I relied more on myself and less on God.

I chose the multitude of details over fellowship with my Shepherd. With no one to stay with my husband, there were many weeks I could not attend church. One rare morning I was able to get out of the house, and it happened to be Communion Sunday. I stood alone and alien-like as the neighborly conversation of others in the foyer swirled around me. My world was falling apart, yet every one of these people seemed carefree.

After the music and sermon, the pastor began preparing for communion. He asked us to pray for forgiveness that we might be ready to receive the elements. Normally, I'd recite a laundry list of sins, but on this occasion I simply tried to still my emotions and spirit. Since God didn't need a recital of the sins He already knew about, I asked the Lord to please show me how I had saddened Him the most.

As the gentle music played in the background, I heard Him whisper, "You simply don't trust me, my child. Don't you realize that nothing is too big for me?" The silent tears began to course down my face as I realized how true this was. Yes, I had problems that seemed immense. Over $10,000 in medical bills, no health insurance, little income, a dying husband, and raising two teenagers virtually alone were gigantic problems. But God is bigger than any problem.

Second Corinthians 12:9 tells us that God's grace is sufficient and His power is made perfect in our weakness. I certainly felt weak that day, but I began to remember His promise to always provide for me. I understood He would unfailingly take what was evil or sad or disastrous in my life and turn it into good for His glory because He knew I loved him.

The myriad of sins I could have uttered died on my lips as I confessed the sin of not trusting God. I had somehow elevated myself to the one who has all the answers. I realized that God never asked me to solve every problem.

He has never asked any of us to be a superman or superwoman. All that God has ever asked and will ever ask is that we trust Him. We need to trust our Shepherd—our provider and caregiver—in every area of our caregiving and every sphere our life, even when it seems He is silent and unconcerned.

Of course it hasn't come easy for me. I know that you, like my friend, Loretta, have also had your share of struggles. After caring for her son for several years, the doctor gave her a warning that in six months Marc would need total care. The doctor's timeline was correct, but Loretta fought the verdict every step of the way.

At a time when expenses were increasing because of Marc's illness, the last thing she needed was to have her income disappear. She bargained with God and tried every conceivable way to have Marc's needs taken care of without having to quit her job. The result of trying to do everything in her own strength was making her physically and emotionally sick. Worse yet, her spiritual health suffered.

In her disobedience and lack of trust, fear filled her life. It wasn't only the money, but the fact that this wasn't what she wanted for her life and certainly not for Marc's. Loretta's breast cancer and mastectomy was the wake-up call she never wanted, but she had no choice but to finally accept life on whatever terms she was given.

When she began caring for her son twenty-four hours a day, Loretta rediscovered Marc's loving nature and his sense of urgency to win as many people to the Lord as possible. Today Marc is no longer the burden she initially worried he would become. He's now a companion. Together they go to movies, the park, and pleasure drives. In the evening after Marc gives the neighbor children a ride on his wheelchair, Loretta reads the cards and letters his friends have sent to him.

Loretta is still watching her son die, but now she is trusting God. In miraculous ways her bills are being paid, and she will never regret the time she is spending with Marc.

According to C. S. Lewis, "Relying on God has to begin all over again every day as if nothing had yet been done." Because God is perfect, He is incapable of letting us down; and His mercies are new every day.

Providence is the care God takes of all existing things.
—Hesychios of Sinai

God gives us strength enough, and sense enough, for everything He wants us to do.
—John Ruskin

And my God will meet all your needs according to his glorious riches in Christ Jesus.
—Philippians 4:19

GREAT IS THY FAITHFULNESS

THOMAS O. CHISHOLM

Great is Thy faithfulness! Great is Thy faithfulness!

Morning by morning new mercies I see.

All I have needed Thy hand hath provided;

Great is Thy faithfulness, Lord, unto me!

CHAPTER THREE

THE SHEPHERD OF *Rest*

"HE MAKES ME LIE DOWN IN GREEN PASTURES"

AFTER THE FIRE

When we first learned the news, I was furious. I wanted to hurt someone, to throw things. I wanted a fix for what was happening. I was by nature and experience a fixer, but there was no fixing this.

Come to me, all you who are weary and burdened, and I will give you rest.
—Matthew 11:28

I knew I should pray. I wanted to pray, but it was easier and less painful to be angry. Prayer was an admission that this fixer, this wonder woman, couldn't do it all. But as long as I kept moving and doing everything on my to-do list, I'd be okay.

Instead of praying, I directed my anger at the doctors

who didn't know anything about this disease that was killing my husband. I snapped at my children and railed at the injustice of it all. I was angry with myself for being so impatient. Forty years on earth had honed me to the point where little bothered me for long, but nothing had prepared me for being a caregiver.

One day after lunch, I threw in a load of laundry and left David sleeping while I went to the grocery store. I stopped for a few other errands and returned about an hour later to a smoke-filled house and the incessant wailing of several ear-piercing alarms. I ducked outside, took in a fresh breath of air, and rushed back in to check on my husband. Amazingly, he slept on, oblivious to the disaster outside the bedroom door.

I ran through the house opening windows and doors. The last place I checked was the laundry room where smoke billowed out from under the closed door. My washing machine was on fire!

The first couple of cycles had gone smoothly, but for some reason the machine was now stuck on agitation. The dial moved forward and backward over and over, causing so much friction that the front panel of the machine exploded into flames. I was able to beat out the fire, turn off the machine, and open the laundry room door leading to the outside. When I knew the house was safe I disconnected the alarms and cried. I sat in my smoky house crying, not only because I needed to buy a new washing machine, but also from exhaustion.

A. J. Gossip said about prayer: "We can do nothing, we say sometimes, we can only pray. That, we feel, is a terribly precarious second-best. So long as we can fuss and work and rush about, so long as we can lend a hand, we have some hope; but if we have to fall back upon God—ah, then things must be critical indeed!"

During my first two years as a caregiver, I was not unlike the washing machine—stuck on agitation and filled with anger and tension. I became disconcerted to the point of bursting into emotional flames. Asking God to help was admitting that the situation was critical. My anger, impatience, and unwillingness to ask for help had made it impossible to rest or pray.

Thankfully, my tears gave way to rest and eventually to prayer. I got a new washing machine and a new attitude so I could survive this terrible disease. After my trial by fire, I learned that I needed to rest not just my body but also my soul. I spent time resting in the assurance that God loved me and would always be there for me. The needed rest I found in my Shepherd didn't change my situation, but it did change me.

Spending time with the Lord the first thing in the morning and the last thing at night mysteriously made me more

productive during the day. Trusting God helped me put away my cares and sleep more soundly. I became less angry, more patient, a more creative problem solver, and better at managing my time.

A caregiver's job is not easy. Many hold full-time jobs and have young children to care for along with other loved ones. Caregiving doesn't mean we don't have to clean or cook or balance the checkbook. It doesn't mean our children can raise themselves or that we will get a paycheck without going to work each day. No, caregiving means our day is consumed with a never-ending list of priorities.

More than a decade ago, Robert Fulghum wrote a best-seller that inspired an entire nation—*All I Really Need to Know I Learned in Kindergarten.* One of the lessons is: "Take a nap every afternoon." Most caregivers I know can't take a nap once a week much less once a day. Not a physical nap at least.

Webster's Dictionary has several definitions for the word *rest*. One definition paints a perfect picture of our Shepherd—*that on which anything rests or leans for support.* I'm so glad that I have God to lean on for support. Aren't you?

Find rest, O my soul, in God alone; my hope comes from him.
—Psalm 62:5

Prayer is a cry of distress, a demand for help, a hymn of love.
—Alexis Carrel

Sometimes the most important thing in a whole day is the rest we take between two deep breaths, or the turning inwards in prayer for five short minutes.
—Etty Hillesum

IN THE GARDEN

—CHARLES AUSTIN MILES

And He walks with me,

and He talks with me,

And He tells me I am His own;

And the joy we share as we tarry there,

None other has ever known.

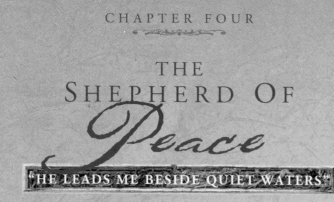

CHAPTER FOUR

THE
SHEPHERD OF
Peace

"HE LEADS ME BESIDE QUIET WATERS"

EIGHT MILES TO PEACE

Before Bob turned sixty, he was diagnosed with a disease similar to Parkinson's. His motor skills failed first, followed by his mental functions. Bob lived independently for a couple of years after diagnosis, then he moved to a senior apartment building, and finally to a nursing home for the last eighteen months of his life.

Do not be anxious about anything, but in everything, by prayer and petition, with thanksgiving, present your requests to God.
—Philippians 4:6

With each move, Bob's speech became more difficult to understand until eventually, only his son, Jim, could make sense of his garbled intonation and small hand gestures. Jim developed patience as he would sit for up to thirty minutes trying to comprehend a simple two-sentence request.

Throughout those last eighteen months, Jim made the twelve-minute drive to the nursing home every Sunday afternoon. Each week as he returned home from seeing his dad, Jim thought and prayed and grieved. Even though Bob had

been an avid fisherman and hunter, he had not always been a model, loveable father. His life had been filled with alcohol and various women; and his success in business was only marginal. To become a caregiver to his father was not a logical or natural step for Jim. True, his dad had been fun loving and cared about the happiness of other people, but Bob's life was not the life Jim chose to emulate when he became a parent. There was not a strong bond between the two men. While they had seen each other sometimes for holidays and talked occasionally, it was usually only when Bob needed money.

Shortly before his father's death, Jim drove home following a meeting with hospice personnel. As he drove, he asked God to make Bob's last days comfortable. Jim found himself thinking of John 14:2, "In my Father's house are many rooms; if it were not so, I would have told you. I am going there to prepare a place for you." Somehow, despite the past, Jim prayed that God would make a place for his father.

Three days later Jim got the call that every caregiver dreads, yet knows will come. The nursing home phoned to tell Jim that his father might not make it through the night. He hopped into the car and drove those eight miles in well under his normal twelve minutes. He ran into his father's room and grabbed his hand. At first his father seemed non-responsive, but then Jim felt a slight squeeze.

Jim sat holding his father's hand as he prayed, "God, please make room for Dad." Bob stopped breathing within two minutes of that simple prayer.

For eighteen months, Jim had driven faithfully to the nursing home, scarcely knowing why. As a follower of Christ, he knew all about honoring his parents. But how about when a parent didn't deserve to be honored? What about all the wrongs that were never made right?

Psalm 29:11 tells us, "The LORD gives strength to his people; the LORD blesses his people with peace." Caregiving was something Jim would never have chosen, yet with each visit, the wrongs of the past didn't seem to matter nearly as much as getting to know his father. What started as a chore turned into a blessing. When Bob stopped breathing, the Shepherd gave Jim peace. He felt sure that his dad was no longer uncomfortable but at home with Him.

Jim marveled that such a loving and forgiving Father had worked so tangibly in his life. He had sped to his father's bedside alone with fear and "what-ifs." Now he drove those eight miles home at a more leisurely pace with God . . . and at peace.

> *In this world, full often, our joys are only the tender shadows which our sorrows cast.*
> —Henry Ward Beecher

> *God cannot give us happiness and peace apart from himself, because it is not there. There is no such thing.*
> —C. S. Lewis

> *And the peace of God, which transcends all understanding, will guard your hearts and your minds in Christ Jesus.*
> —Philippians 4:7

IT IS WELL WITH MY SOUL

—HORATIO G. SPAFFORD

When peace, like a river, attendeth my way,

When sorrows like sea billows roll;

Whatever my lot, Thou has taught me to say,

It is well, it is well, with my soul.

CHAPTER FIVE

THE SHEPHERD OF
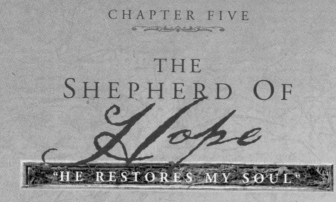

Hope

"HE RESTORES MY SOUL"

GOOD-BYE KISSES

Tricia spent her first four years living with her mom and her grandparents. She was the first grandchild and the recipient of her grandparents' adoring attention. After her mom married, Tricia always lived within a few miles of her grandparents' house. Sundays, after school, and every holiday were spent with Grammy and Papa.

Now faith is being sure of what we hope for and certain of what we do not see.
—Hebrews 11:1

Even after Tricia married John and had three children, Tricia still spent as much time as possible with her grandparents. But when God called Tricia and John to move one thousand miles from California to Montana, she worried about not being near her grandparents. Her greatest fear was that she'd get a call telling her one of them had passed away.

Tricia suggested the elderly couple move to Montana, but her grandmother refused. She'd lived in the same town her whole life and wasn't about to move away from her friends

and all that was safe and familiar. That changed when her grandfather was diagnosed with a terminal illness. Even after surgery the doctor wasn't hopeful, but her grandfather chose to forgo aggressive therapies. He was eighty-three, ready to go, and he didn't want any more treatments. But there was one thing he did want—he wanted to move to Montana and be with his Tricia.

It took three snow-filled days to make the thousand-mile trip to Montana. Her grandfather never complained as he and Tricia's grandmother moved their belongings to their new home.

Tricia was a writer, a homeschooling mom, and now she took on the job of caregiver. For three months there were doctor visits, trips to the pharmacy, and visits from hospice. She spent as much time as possible with her grandfather, sitting and talking with him, listening to his stories about growing up in Kansas, and cooking his favorite foods. Tricia's efforts were a payback for the lavish love her grandparents had shown her over the years.

He got weaker by the day. He had to be helped to the restroom; he couldn't walk without support. Tricia knew the end was coming. How would she handle it? How could she deal with losing someone who meant so much?

Knowing she could never face the end by herself, she turned to God. She spent time reading the Bible and seeking comfort. She poured over everything the Bible had to say to her about heaven. There she found hope that this man, who had never wavered in his love for her, would soon be in the presence of Christ.

During his last few weeks Tricia read scriptures to him and felt the Lord's presence in the room. It was as if God was right there as He eagerly anticipated taking this saint home, as if angels were reading over her shoulder.

Days before her grandfather's passing, Tricia went upstairs and entered her grandparents' bedroom. Both of these dear Christians were in tears. Her sweet, quiet grandfather was sobbing with his frail arms raised. He said over and over, "Thank you, Lord Jesus. I love you, Lord Jesus."

Not knowing what had happened to bring about the

tears, Tricia sat and prayed with them both. Later, she asked her grandmother what had happened.

"I was reading to Grandpa," she explained. "He had been looking out the window and he interrupted me and said, 'Dear, do you smell that? That's the most wonderful smell I've ever experienced.'

"Well, a few minutes later he said, 'Look, Dear, see all those birds out the window? Look at those beautiful white birds.' Soon he said, 'And look at that lion. I've never seen something so beautiful. If I were an artist, I would love to paint that lion.'" Sobs and praises interrupted his words.

"I saw Jesus," said the frail old man. "His arms were outstretched and welcoming," he continued, lifting his hands to show how Jesus was reaching toward him. That was the last day he spoke.

The following day was his final day awake. Grandfather and granddaughter had always blown kisses to each other. While he lived with Tricia, they'd continued to do this throughout the day, every time she'd leave his room. During his last waking moment, her grandfather blew her a kiss. He couldn't say goodbye, but his kiss said it all. Tricia knew it would be the last one.

Jane L. Weaver said, "Delicate threads of hope, patiently woven, become the strong fabric of our faith." When the time came, Tricia's hope, woven over the years, made a strong fabric of faith to help her say good-bye. Because of that faith, she knew her beloved grandfather was in a better place. He was now at peace.

Caring for a loved one is one of the most difficult things we might be called to do. It can also be one of the most fulfilling. The Shepherd's hope can sustain us and turn caregiving into a gift.

According to Herman Melville, "Hope is the struggle of the soul, breaking loose from what is perishable, and attesting her eternity." As her grandfather's soul struggled to break loose from his perishable body, the Shepherd was there to welcome him to eternity. One day he'll welcome Tricia home, too.

Our hope begins and ends in God, the source of all hope.
—Mary Lou Redding

Hope is not the conviction that something will turn out well but the certainty that something makes sense, regardless of how it turns out.
—Vaclav Havel

Be strong and take heart, all you who hope in the LORD.
—Psalm 31:24

NEAR TO THE HEART OF GOD

—CLELAND B. MCAFEE

There is a place of quiet rest,

Near to the heart of God.

A place where sin cannot molest,

Near to the heart of God.

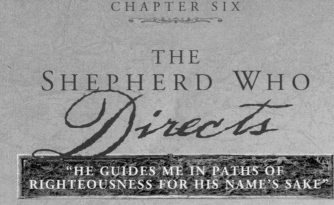

CHAPTER SIX

THE SHEPHERD WHO *Directs*

"HE GUIDES ME IN PATHS OF RIGHTEOUSNESS FOR HIS NAME'S SAKE"

THE LIFE I HAD PLANNED

One thing I know about myself is that I don't like being around sick people. I was one of eight children, and my mother did not have time for sickness. In fact, we were each allowed one sick day a year. I always thought that if someone is sick—get drugs and get better. If that doesn't work, then please have the good grace to die.

Can you think of anyone more ill-equipped to be a caregiver than me? The day David received his diagnosis we held each other as I assured him that I was in this for

I will instruct you and teach you in the way you should go; I will counsel you and watch over you.
—Psalm 32:8

the long haul. But that night, after David went to sleep, the true me took over as I screamed out my silent rage.

I went to my pastor expecting direction. I wanted a plan. I wanted him to tell me how to make it all go away so life would be normal. Instead he said, "I know you don't want to hear what I have to say, but I can see beyond where you are now. I will read the books you will write, hear the songs you will sing, and see the groups to which you will speak."

His statement did nothing to lift my wretchedness, and I left the office feeling more bereft than I had ever felt in my life. On top of the sadness and grief, I was filled with anger. I did not want to see beyond where I was. I wanted to go back to where I had been before we learned the devastating news.

At a convention almost a year after the diagnosis, I presented an essay about my current struggles as a caregiver. After the presentation, people surrounded me saying, "May I have a copy of your story? I want to give it to my counselor, my doctor, my wife, my pastor, my friends." I had put my grief into words, and people could identify with my feelings of hurt and anger, loss and fear.

Nothing is ever wasted in God's economy. He uses our

gifts for a purpose far larger than we could possibly imagine. Joseph Campbell said, "We must be willing to get rid of the life we have planned, so as to have the life that is awaiting us." Getting rid of the life I had planned was easy because it happened overnight without my consent. Learning to accept the new life was more difficult, but eventually I looked to the Shepherd for direction.

Since David's diagnosis in 1994, I have started both local and online support groups, established a nationwide speaking ministry, created a Website, and written two books about people who are dealing with David's disease.

Understanding the disease process and reaching out to assist others moved me from denial and depression to eventual acceptance. As I reached my breaking point, I realized I couldn't control everything and gave my Shepherd room to work.

Mary's direction from the Shepherd led her to caring for her adult son, John. He was a happily married Vietnam veteran until a vein ruptured in his brain in 1978. Ten years later, a second episode landed him in the hospital for an experimental procedure. The surgery saved John's life but threw his wife into the role of caregiver. They settled into a routine and though it wasn't what either of them had planned, it was the way things were.

Caregiving eventually took a toll on John's marriage, leading to divorce for he and his wife. On December 31, 1993, John finally had to move into a nursing home because he was unable to take care of himself.

Charles Stanley said, "As you walk through the valley of the unknown, you will find the footprints of Jesus both in front of you and beside you." This was true for John, but his mother's footprints have been there, too.

Because there were no other care options for John, Mary decided being in a nursing home didn't have to mean being alone. For over ten years, Mary has been a constant visitor for her son and the other residents as well. What started out as a mother's love has become a ministry.

Mary has become an unpaid member of the nursing home care team. She decorates for holidays, plans and orchestrates games and other activities, and fills in wherever needed.

Neither Mary nor John could have predicted that their

lives would revolve around a nursing home. Residents and staff admire Mary and marvel at her selfless devotion to her son and hundreds of others.

Psalm 119:105 tells us that God's word is a lamp at our feet and a light for our path no matter how dark it seems outside. Our Shepherd has a perfect sense of direction and as long as we follow Him, we will too.

When a train goes through a tunnel and it gets
dark, you don't throw away the ticket and jump off.
You sit still and trust the engineer.
—Corrie Ten Boom

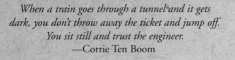

It is only in misery
that we recognize
the hand of God
leading good
men to good.
—Johann Wolfgang
Von Goeth

Whether you turn to the right or to the left, your ears will hear
a voice behind you, saying, "This is the way; walk in it."
—Isaiah 30:21

AMAZING GRACE

—JOHN NEWTON

Through many dangers, toils and snares,

I have already come;

'Tis grace hath brought me safe thus far,

And grace will lead me home.

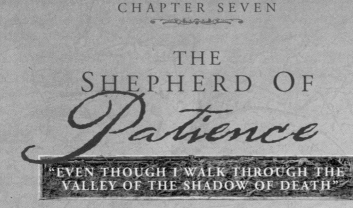

CHAPTER SEVEN

THE SHEPHERD OF Patience

> "EVEN THOUGH I WALK THROUGH THE VALLEY OF THE SHADOW OF DEATH"

LOOKING FOR A YELLOW WALL

When Gerri and Charlie first married, the love, commitment, and dedication implicit in the words *husband* and *wife* were powerful and intoxicating. So much so, that from the beginning, Charlie called her "Wife," and she called him "Husband."

"Hello, Wife," he'd say, when he called from work.

"Welcome home, Husband," she'd respond when he came through the door.

You need to persevere so that when you have done the will of God, you will receive what he has promised.
—Hebrews 10:36

They used their given names too, and on rare occasions, a name or two better left unsaid, but these words, Husband and Wife, were their touchstones. In the middle of an emotional moment or disagreement, if one of them used these special terms, they were instantly reminded of their love and their vows.

As Charlie began his slide into illness, everything changed. He began to fixate and tell Gerri how she had ruined his life. His rages always ended with him screaming, "I hate you! I hate you!" Day after day, month after month, any effort on Gerri's part ended with screaming matches and verbal abuse and often physical threats or even actions.

What had started out with such joy turned into a living nightmare. Where was the husband she had married with such hope? The illness was having a devastating effect on Charlie, making him behave as he did. And the strain on Gerri was clear to anyone who saw her.

One day, after ringing up her order, a convenience store clerk said, "I hope your day gets better." Gerri had not said one word, but the strain was obvious even to someone who had never met her.

After hearing Gerri lament her situation yet another time, an old friend asked, "Why do you keep painting the wall blue and expecting it to be yellow?" Gerri's friend had summed up the situation perfectly. The old Charlie, the prior-to-sickness Charlie was the yellow wall that Gerri wanted in her home, yet it was the blue wall she faced each day.

Gerri realized that she would need the proverbial patience of Job to continue loving Charlie. Instead of going through the same actions and arguments with him and expecting a different outcome, she had to accept the reality.

Another friend, Jean, is further along in her caregiving journey. She also had her years of looking for a yellow wall and only seeing blue. In fact, for a period of time, she saw divorce as the only solution. Because her husband, Don, did and said so many hurtful things, she came to the point of almost hating him. For many years she just went through the motions of being a wife. But they recently celebrated their thirtieth anniversary. God had gradually brought love for her husband back into her heart even after all they had gone through to get to the special day.

After Don entered the nursing home, things changed.

Jean found that the time she now spends with him isn't stressful or combative. Prior to the nursing care she stated, "I know the day-to-day caregiving was killing my soul and body." No, their relationship is not like it was in the early, fun years, but when she tells Don, "I love you," she sincerely means it.

For many years, my least favorite Bible verse was James 1:2–3. I wouldn't be surprised if Gerri and Jean and other caregivers feel the same way. This passage tells us to, "Consider it pure joy . . . whenever you face trials of many kinds, because you know that the testing of your faith develops perseverance."

I liked the faith part of that verse. I wanted to be a woman of faith. I wanted people to marvel at how I trusted God in every area of my life. I didn't, however, want the trials that seem to go hand in hand with the faith. I certainly didn't consider it pure joy to face trials; and I didn't want to have to develop patience. I didn't even like the synonyms for patience I found in the dictionary—resignation, fortitude, forbearance, and longsuffering.

I preferred Barbara Johnson's definition. "Patience is the ability to idle your motor when you feel like stripping your gears." In fact, if the truth were told, I was more like

Margaret Thatcher when she quipped, "I am extraordinarily patient provided I get my own way in the end."

Like Gerri and Jean, having patience and accepting my new role helped me be a better caregiver. The Shepherd was with me during the gear-stripping times. When considering the job of a caregiver, my friend, Cecilia, said, "God keeps one hand around our shoulders and His other hand over our mouths." As long as we lean into the Shepherd's arm and don't pry His hand off our mouth, we'll handle whatever happens, even when we don't get our own way.

Have patience with all things, but chiefly have patience with yourself.
—Francois de Sales

God, grant me the serenity to accept the people I cannot change;
The courage to change the one I can;
And the wisdom to know that person is me.
—Serenity Prayer Variation

I will give you a new heart and put a new spirit in you;
I will remove from you your heart of stone
and give you a heart of flesh.
—Ezekiel 36:26

JUST A CLOSER WALK WITH THEE

—AUTHOR UNKNOWN

I am weak, but Thou art strong;

Jesus, keep me from all wrong;

I'll be satisfied as long

As I walk, let me walk close to Thee.

CHAPTER EIGHT

THE SHEPHERD OF *Courage*

"I WILL FEAR NO EVIL"

A MOTHER'S COURAGE

"Do whatever it takes to save her life," Linda sobbed as she looked down at her semi-conscious seven-and-a-half-year-old daughter.

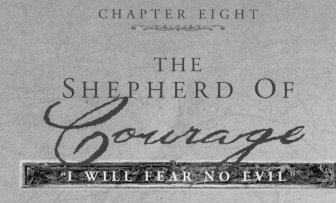

Be strong and coura-geous. Do not be afraid or terrified because of them, for the LORD your God goes with you; he will never leave you nor forsake you.
—Deuteronomy 31:6

"Your daughter is very sick and will die without treatment," explained the young doctor as he listened to the soft hiss of the respirator helping Laura to breathe.

The doctor meant well, but Linda never wavered. Despite what others might say she was no more ready to say good-bye now than she had been six years earlier.

On December 26, 1987, Linda, her mother, and

18-month-old Laura had been in an accident during a sudden rain storm. Linda walked away uninjured. Her mother suffered a broken nose and a cracked pelvis. Laura, however, sustained a head injury which left her in a ten-month-long coma and caused severe handicaps.

Though Laura was not brain dead, the doctors gave her no hope and suggested pulling the plug on her life-support systems. Linda refused. Now a minor bladder infection had suddenly turned into a deadly blood illness, and Laura's life hovered on the brink of death. Linda desperately needed courage from God to fight against the odds as she had done in 1987.

"This illness could be a gift from God," suggested the doctor. "Maybe this is your chance to say goodbye to her."

Linda could understand how some people would think a vent-dependent child requiring twenty-four-hour nursing care might be better off dead, but she also knew her daughter was a joyful child.

"Do whatever it takes to save her life," Linda repeated.

"Your daughter is so disabled. Maybe it's time to let her go. This may be God's way of giving you that opportunity."

Without hesitation Linda again answered no, only to

have the doctor plead his case a final time. Though her daughter had multiple handicaps, Linda found immense pleasure and joy just being with her daughter. Linda's no-nonsense answer put an end to the discussion. The doctor walked away convinced that whatever effort he put forth would, in the long run, be a waste.

Two days later Linda sat next to her daughter in ICU. The infection was leaving Laura's body. She was not only awake and cognitive, but singing as her mother held her hand. The doctor entered the room and saw Linda's joy. He sat down on the edge of her bed and looked up at Linda, tears streaming down his cheeks. He simply said, "I'm so sorry; I didn't know." Linda's courage and unwavering faith in God's timing had once again saved her daughter's life.

Another mother's courage saved her little boy when doctors said nothing could be done. After a difficult pregnancy and delivery, doctors and nurses assured Melina that her baby, Tommy, was fine. At fifteen months old, despite those assurances, he wasn't walking or progressing properly, and was constantly falling head first onto the floor from a sitting position. Over the next three years everyone said the boy was fine, but Melina knew she had to find a way to help her son.

After shuttling between military doctors and bases, Melina found the beginning of hope in Germany where her family was stationed. During a four-hour drive to the hospital for yet another consultation, she prayed to God for courage to find help for Tommy. The visit ended with Melina losing her temper and the doctor refusing to treat her son. They say that hell has no fury like a woman scorned, and the hospital inspector-general probably felt the same way about this mother with a sick child. That righteous anger led Melina to a doctor who gave her a diagnosis and her first ray of hope.

Still, the parade of doctors, occupational therapists, and physical therapists said the same thing: "He'll never walk more than a few steps independently, never graduate from school, and will always be dependent on you for everything."

When Tommy was seven, a doctor finally agreed with Melina that seizures were, in part, responsible for the little boy's falls. She recommended additional tests. Two hours into the procedure, the phone rang at the nurse's station. The neurologist told Melina that Tommy had gone into a series of grand mal seizures that lasted for almost an hour. The young boy now lay in a coma.

Melina hung up the phone, went into the bathroom across the hall, and got down on her knees and prayed to the Shepherd, "Oh dear Jesus, please take care of my son. You have brought Tommy so far."

Returning to her son, Melina sat by his head and began to pray over him and into his ears. The doctors, now three of them, became more concerned as the hours passed with Tommy oblivious to anything going on around him.

Eleven hours had passed since Tommy had slipped into a comatose state, yet Melina continued talking, singing his favorite songs, and most of all, praying. Melina's head was on her son's chest, facing away from him. She felt a touch and slowly turned toward Tommy. His eyes were open, and he was smiling. His little hands reached out and whispered, "Mommy."

Years of surgery, medications, therapy, and a mother's courage made a difference. Today twenty-one-year-old Tommy has been seizure-free without medication for seven years. He drives to the store where he stocks groceries. His next goal is to attend college.

Linda and Melina both became caregivers but never stopped being mothers. Both of these courageous women placed their children in the Shepherd's hands. When we place everything in the Shepherd's hands we can expect our prayers to be answered—sometimes on earth, sometimes in Heaven, but always in wondrous ways.

Courage is the first of human qualities because it is the quality which guarantees all others.
—Winston Churchill

You gain strength, courage and confidence by every experience in which you really stop to look fear in the face. You are able to say to yourself, "I lived through this horror. I can take the next thing that comes along."
—Eleanor Roosevelt

Have I not commanded you? Be strong and courageous. Do not be terrified; do not be discouraged, for the LORD your God will be with you wherever you go.
—Joshua 1:9

I Surrender All

—Judson Wheeler Van DeVenter

I surrender all,

I surrender all,

All to Thee, my blessed Savior,

I surrender all.

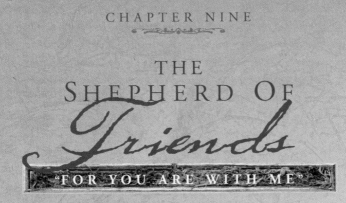

CHAPTER NINE

THE SHEPHERD OF *Friends*

"FOR YOU ARE WITH ME"

BUTTERFLIES AND FRIENDS

"But it's so far," cried eighty-five-year-old Gilda upon hearing Cherie's news.

Cherie gave a reassuring smile as she hugged her elderly neighbor. "We'll still be here. We'll be exactly twenty houses away from you, Gilda." The octogenarian cried despite Cherie's assurance that she would still be there for Gilda and her husband, Gasper.

"A friend loves at all times, and a brother is born for adversity."
—Proverbs 17:17

Five years earlier, Gasper and Gilda had moved from Manhattan to Florida to be close to their daughter. Their advanced age made driving dangerous and mass transportation was almost non-existent. Cherie often saw the couple. They reminded her of Jack Sprat and his wife as they waited for the senior's bus to the grocery store or Wal-Mart. Cherie, in her gentle way, would flash her Miss America smile as she would stop to offer them a ride. The proud pair, reluctant to give up their independence, would wave her by. Eventually they accepted her offer, and the random rides became routine. Before she knew it, Cherie had adopted a set of grandparents.

As the months turned into years, the three transplanted Floridians grew to love each other. What started as an occasional trip to the doctor or market turned into a friendship of immense value for Cherie. "I am getting so much more than I could ever give," she insisted.

A trip to McDonald's for ice cream or to Wendy's for "beans," as Gasper called chili, made their week complete. During those feasts or one of the three weekly trips to the supermarket, Cherie listened to stories of their rich, Italian heritage. Without Cherie's companionship and rides, Gilda and Gasper would not have fared as well. Like many elderly people, they didn't need much help to continue living in their home. They needed more than a caregiver, they needed friends.

Warren Wiersbe said, "Never underestimate the importance of simply being physically present in the place God wants you. You may not be asked to perform some dramatic ministry, but simply being there is a ministry." Cherie doesn't call being in their lives a ministry but that's exactly what it is—the ministry of friendship.

Pastors are often a friend to caregivers, and that's what Pastor Bob was when Christian was dying. He supported Christian's parents as their six-year-old son lay in the hospital knowing his young life was at an end.

It was springtime in Tulsa, the time of the annual invasion of butterflies. Every year for two or three weeks, massive swarms of butterflies descend on Tulsa. They only stay a few days and then disappear overnight to journey on.

In the last week of Christian's life someone brought him one of the butterflies, captured in a jar. Christian held the jar for a few moments, watching the trapped Monarch beating its wings against the glass. With a voice barely above a whisper, he turned to his mother, Marcia. "Mommy, I don't want to keep this butterfly in a jar. He's like me; I'm trapped in a sick body and he's trapped in a jar. Mommy, please let him go free."

Marcia opened the window to his hospital room and took the lid off the jar. The brightly colored, yellow butterfly paused a moment, then took wing and flew out the window. A smile crossed Christian's face, then he sighed, "Mommy, pretty soon I'm going to fly like that butterfly all the way up to heaven."

Nothing Pastor Bob could do or say would change the situation, but he did what he knew to do. He stayed with the family. He was a friend.

About a week later, Christian died in his sleep. Following the funeral, a friend and Pastor Bob accompanied the grieving parents back to their home in the country outside Tulsa. They had been out of their home for several weeks and dreaded going back to the empty house, especially walking back into Christian's room. What could the pastor possibly say to make the situation slightly better?

As they turned the corner and entered their country lane, an amazing sight greeted them. The front lawn of their home was covered with a carpet of brightly-colored butterflies. It was all the more incredible because the butterflies had left Tulsa more than a week before.

As Marcia got out of the car and walked across the lawn, the butterflies scattered. The air was filled with a frenzied riot of color. One of the butterflies separated from the others and came to rest on Marcia's nose. It stayed there for what seemed like an eternity, gently caressing her face with its wings. Then it flew off into the skies toward the heavens.

Marcia, her face aglow, turned and said she felt that God had just given this message: "Marcia, Christian has escaped from his sick body and has flown like a butterfly to heaven."

On that day, the small group at Christian's home saw a miracle of God's grace. That butterfly was a gift from a friend, the Shepherd.

We don't always want answers or advice. Sometimes we just want company.
—Roberta Israeloff

Sometimes the Shepherd calls His people to be friends to those who are caregiving. Friends like Cherie and Pastor Bob, following God's call, can be a tremendous support during difficult times. Sometimes, however, only the Shepherd can befriend the hurting in such a way to give them the peace that passes all understanding.

Thus nature has no love for solitude, and always leans, as it were, on some support; and the sweetest support is found in the most intimate friendship.
—Cicero

Carry each other's burdens, and in this way you will fulfill the law of Christ.
—Galatians 6:2

WHAT A FRIEND WE HAVE IN JESUS

—JOSEPH MEDLICOTT SCRIVEN

What a Friend we have in Jesus, all our sins and griefs to bear!

What a privilege to carry everything to God in prayer!

O what peace we often forfeit, O what needless pain we bear,

All because we do not carry everything to God in prayer.

THE
SHEPHERD WHO
Comforts

"YOUR ROD AND YOUR STAFF, THEY COMFORT ME"

TWO PACKAGES

My friend, Diane, married her childhood sweetheart and quickly started a family. Her husband, Vince, drove a truck on a scheduled route.

For years, before heading out on his route on Monday, no matter how late he was, he always remembered to fill Diane's van. Pumping gas was one of those little things Diane hated to do. And Vince, in a show of his love, would laugh about how his bride didn't need to smell gas anyway.

Praise be to . . . the God of all comfort, who comforts us in all our troubles, so that we can comfort those in any trouble with the comfort we ourselves have received from God.
—2 Corinthians 1:3, 4

For twenty years, Diane basked in Vince's love and devotion.

When Diane looked at Vince, she saw "happily ever after" with a smile in his eyes and a grin on his lips. It was a busy life for the two of them. Never enough money and the ups and downs of raising six children, but Diane and Vince still found time to sneak away for walks to reconnect with each other.

Today, Diane is more than a mother and wife; she is a caregiver for her husband. She recently received guardianship for the man who was her protector for twenty years, and though there were no other options, another piece of her heart broke off that day.

With five children still at home, Diane has little time to spend with friends who live in her town. She does, however, take advantage of the empty evenings to interact with a group of women she has met on the Internet.

In the Shepherd's perfect timing, when she was at her lowest, these friends sent Diane an unusual, comforting gift. One woman on Diane's email discussion list asked some of her friends to individually knit one afghan square. Each of the women who had never met Diane, mailed her square to the friend who pieced them together to make a present, fashioned with love.

"We knew you were having a hard time. We wanted to

wrap you in love, comfort, and prayers," said the note included with the afghan. For the first time in several years tears of joy trickled down Diane's cheeks as she wrapped herself in the tangible evidence of the Shepherd's comfort.

The Shepherd's comfort goes beyond national boundaries, too. Cecilia lives in Namibia. Her husband, Steve, had the same disease as my husband, David. She first contacted me after reading my posting on an Internet message board. I didn't know if she was a Christian; however, I did know God had brought her into my life from the other side of the world. I responded with a comforting message, letting her know that as a caregiver I understood her pain and frustrations.

Later that day, a friend mentioned her son's mission trip to Namibia. Most Americans have never heard of this remote southwest African country on the Atlantic Ocean. Yet here was someone I knew who needed comfort in Namibia at the very time that a church was planning a mission trip there. My friend, Linda, contacted Sylvia, the pastor's wife in Namibia, to arrange for someone to visit.

Cecilia had had no contact with anyone else dealing with the specific problems of this type of caregiving since he was the only person in the entire country afflicted with this disease.

Cecilia rejoiced at the news of the upcoming visit and the care package filled with books, pamphlets, and other information I was sending. Her hope and strength were renewed as her sense of isolation was being diminished. She knew I cared. Better still, she knew the Shepherd cared and would be a constant comfort to her no matter what.

Webster's Dictionary defines comfort as "giving hope in a time of grief or pain, to make something less severe or more bearable." This is exactly what happened. Two comforting packages, delivered from two separate cyberspace connections orchestrated by the Shepherd, made a difference for two wives.

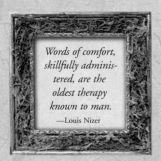

Words of comfort, skillfully administered, are the oldest therapy known to man.
—Louis Nizer

The foundation of the Christian's peace is everlasting; it is what no time, no change can destroy. It will remain when the body dies; it will remain when the mountains depart and the hills shall be removed, and when the heavens shall be rolled together as a scroll. The fountain of His comfort shall never be diminished, and the stream shall never be dried. His comfort and joy is a living spring in the soul, a well of water springing up to everlasting life.
—Jonathan Edwards

Blessed are they who mourn, for they shall be comforted.
—Matthew 5:4

BLESSED ASSURANCE

—FANNY CROSBY

Perfect submission, all is at rest

I in my Savior am happy and blest,

Watching and waiting, looking above,

Filled with His goodness, lost in His love.

CHAPTER ELEVEN

THE
SHEPHERD OF
Protection

"YOU PREPARE A TABLE BEFORE ME IN THE PRESENCE OF MY ENEMIES"

THE SQUEAKY WHEEL

How was I going to take care of my husband without insurance or money? Everywhere I turned the answer was no. I'd cut through all the red tape, worked through mountains of paperwork, and used every conceivable loophole. Hospice had been a blessing, but even that was coming to an end. All the programs I'd unearthed were for people over sixty-five. David wasn't even fifty yet. How would I manage?

But you are a shield around me, O LORD; you bestow glory on me and lift up my head.
—Psalm 3:3

One night as I slept, David began hitting me on the face

as he tried to kill the spiders coming out of my head.

"Stop it! There aren't any spiders!" I said.

"Spiders! They're everywhere. Kill them, kill them!" This frail man who had replaced my husband inflicted a rain of stinging blows. In his tortured mind there were thousands of spiders crawling all over me.

After a vicious slap to the ear, I grabbed my pillow and a blanket and slammed the bedroom door. Huddling on the sofa, I raged at God. How could He allow this to happen? I'd played by the rules and done everything possible. Where was His protection?

To top it off, the next morning the nurse arrived to *release* David from hospice. He'd been on the program for six months, but there had been no significant decline. Nothing I said made a difference. Rules were rules; he was to be released. After I explained what had happened the night before, she suggested I call the doctor and have him tweak the medication. I calmly explained why a mere tweak wouldn't work. She agreed to call the doctor and ask him to admit David so his medications could be adjusted in a safe environment.

My respite was short lived. Two days and countless tests later, they decided he was no danger to himself or me.

Strange thoughts began going through my mind: *What if I didn't pick him up? What if I hopped on a plane to Hawaii, joined my children, and we started our lives over?*

Several scenarios later, I knew I could never abandon David. It wasn't his fault he was sick. With a resolute sigh, I drove to the hospital praying that somehow a solution could be found. There just had to be a way I could take care of my husband without losing myself.

The social worker slid a sheaf of papers across the desk and told me she would have David taken to the lobby after we were done.

"What would happen if I didn't sign these papers and I left David here?" I asked. I hadn't planned it, but once the words came out, they seemed right.

"It doesn't work that way," said Ms. By-The-Book, ruler of her domain. "This isn't a hotel."

"What would happen, though, if I walked out of here and got hit by a truck? Would you find a place for David to live, one that would give him the care he needs?"

"But you didn't get hit by a truck. You're fine. Just sign the papers."

I knew this was the answer I had prayed for, as unorthodox as it was. I knew the system could take care of David.

I would help, but I couldn't do it by myself any longer.

"You have two choices," I told the astonished woman. "You can tell David that I got hit by a truck and died, and I'll walk away and you can pick up the pieces. Or, you can tell him that together we have found a lovely home for him and that I'll come visit him every day and spend time with him and the other residents. When you decide, give me call."

On quivering legs, I walked out of the room with head held high. Would she call my bluff? Silence followed me as I made it down the hall, into the elevator, and finally to the van. Like a giddy child free on a snow day, I decided to play. For the first time in years I was alone, seemingly, with no obligations. I treated myself to lunch and a movie and a little window-shopping. As the clock flew towards quitting time, I knew I had to face the inevitable.

Sure enough, when I got home there were messages. Lots of them—from the social worker, the doctor, the administrator, and even the hospice nurse. Though they were only doing their jobs, to me they were the enemy. The burdens that had been lifted from my shoulders during my carefree afternoon came crashing down heavier than before.

Then came the last message, "Would you be able to visit

Island Lake and see if it's suitable for your husband?"

With that one question it was as if God had reached down and lifted those heavy burdens. Then he wrapped his loving arms around me and helped me dial the phone. That old adage about the squeaky wheel getting the grease was true. I'd squeaked and a team worked together on what had seemed an unsolvable problem.

That same evening, David slept in his new bed a mere fifteen minutes away. Despite waiting lists at every nursing home in the area, he had a bed. I'd never signed the hospice discharge papers, and David had received special treatment because of his terminal status.

What could have been my Waterloo of battles turned into victory with the Shepherd's help. Once David was admitted, Medicaid was approved, and I no longer had to pay for his medications out of pocket. The best part was that my husband, this man I had promised to take care of no matter what, got the care he needed and our time together wasn't spent in fear or anger.

The Shepherd protected David and me and led us to a nursing home filled with caring staff. There were more battles to fight, like the feeding tube and the expensive wheelchair, but with God's help we got everything David needed.

Eleanor Roosevelt said, "You must do the thing you think you cannot do." I didn't think I could continue to care for David, but God knew that with His help I could. And I did.

Not everything that is faced can be changed, but nothing can be changed until it is faced.
—James Baldwin

As sure as God puts His children into the furnace of affliction, He will be with them in it.
—Charles Spurgeon

When you pass through the waters, I will be with you; and when you pass through the rivers, they will not sweep over you. When you walk through the fire, you will not be burned; the flames will not set you ablaze.
—Isaiah 43:2

A MIGHTY FORTRESS IS OUR GOD

—MARTIN LUTHER

A mighty fortress is our God, a bulwark never failing;

Our helper He, amid the flood of mortal ills prevailing:

For still our ancient foe doth seek to work us woe;

His craft and power are great, and armed with cruel hate,

On earth is not his equal.

CHAPTER TWELVE

THE SHEPHERD WHO *Heals*

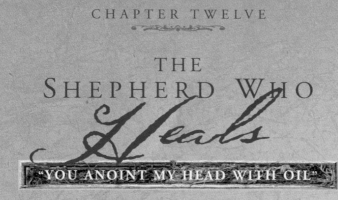

"YOU ANOINT MY HEAD WITH OIL"

THREADS OF LAUGHTER

"Your husband would be healed if it wasn't for sin in your life," said a well-meaning friend one day when I was out shopping.

He heals the broken-hearted and binds up their wounds.
—Psalm 147:3

I could not believe what I was hearing. My husband was in a state of progressive decline from an incurable disease and my sin was the problem? With no scriptural references to support her theory, I found fault with her reasoning. Besides, even though he did have a serious disease, he could still do some things. Couldn't he?

Folding the laundry, washing dishes, cleaning a toilet,

or even screwing in a light bulb seemed beyond his ability. It wasn't that he lacked the willingness to help, he simply did an appalling job of each chore. I truly understood each mistake, each broken dish, each unmade bed. Yet the growing seeds of discontent had taken hold and were beginning to flourish. I caught the sharp words of my rebuke after they slipped from my lips. I listened to my heavy sighs of exasperation and found myself rolling my eyes in disgust.

One morning I prayed that I might accept David and his inabilities. "Please, Lord. Give me just one reason to rejoice in my husband." I dragged myself into the shower where the sharp spray would relax my aching body. I reached for the soap and paused in thought. There are two things I can't stand. One is finding only a sliver of soap once I am wet; the second is finding no toilet paper when I need it. I stood amazed in the shower realizing God had answered my prayer. I had asked for just one thing that David could still do. In an instant God had shown me two.

In the three years we had been married, I'd never replaced a bar of soap or the toilet tissue. I'd taken for granted that they were always there when I needed them. As much as David couldn't do, there were things he could do.

No, it wasn't my sin that was preventing David from being healed, but I needed healing for my attitude. I thought about what had drawn me to David in the first place and our ability to laugh together was at the top of the list. It had been a long time since we had shared any laughter.

I knew there was no way I could repair what was broken; only God could do that. I believed that God could heal David, but until He chose to do so, I figured if I couldn't fix it I might as well laugh at it.

Soon, an impeccable house didn't seem nearly as important as catching a comedy at the local theater. There would come a day when I could no longer transport David, and besides, the chores would always be there.

I bought joke books and perused the Internet looking for funny stories and classic humor. I worked at finding the funny in every situation and enlisted the aid of my children and friends. As my disposition improved, there seemed less time to worry. What Dwight D. Eisenhower said was true, "Laughter can relieve tension, soothe the pain of disappointment, and strengthen the spirit for the formidable tasks that always lie ahead." There was no doubt that a formidable task lay ahead, but somehow the laughter, and even simple smiles, changed our situation. I found out that smiles and laughter are excellent seamstresses.

Watching David decline and seeing the end of our

dreams tore my heart into tiny pieces. Each drop in ability and every compromise rent the fabric of our lives. Our smiles became the thread that mended our hearts. Laughter sewed together pieces of sadness and wove a safety net that would rescue us again and again when the unthinkable happened one more time.

One evening we found humor in a game of Monopoly. The game was going smoothly until my younger son, Justin, in a characteristically capitalistic move, wanted to buy several properties from his brother. This coup, if he could coerce his brother into selling, would give him a monopoly—one entire city block.

This was bad news for the other three players in the game; I was perilously close to bankruptcy. Justin offered his brother an obscene amount of money, to no avail. When that didn't work, he switched to incentives, including, "You'll never have to pay me rent if you land on these." Nicholas, child of my heart during that hard fought Monopoly game, persisted in saying, "No."

Finally, Justin looked at his brother, often the source of much conflict and jealously in his life, and smiled. "Please let me buy them from you, Nicholas. If you do, I'll love you forever."

Nicholas' face melted, and we all broke into laughter. Their completed transaction soon forced me into bankruptcy, and the game eventually ended with Justin the undisputed real estate mogul, despite not charging his brother rent.

Our laughter knit a cloak to protect our love for one another, and we still laugh about that game. Somehow, despite everything, the laughter helped us to retain our family oneness.

The very reason you're a caregiver—love for someone else—has ripped your world apart and, if you're like me, you need to be mended. We all want our loved ones to be healed on this earth when the reality is that sometimes the healing we pray for takes place in Heaven.

One of my favorite depictions of Jesus is when children surround him. His head is thrown back and He is laughing in such a way that you know it's a belly laugh. We've all heard the verse in proverbs that reminds us that a merry heart is like good medicine. *Are you taking your medicine?*

Laughter is the tonic, the relief, the surcease for pain.
—Charlie Chaplin

Humor alone can't take away the grief, restore finances, or change the situation, but it can surely soften the blow. Once we find laughter, no matter what comes next, we can survive it.

Good humor is tonic for the mind and body. It is the best antidote for anxiety and depression. It lightens human burdens. It is the direct route to serenity and contentment.
—Grenville Kleiser

A time to weep and a time to laugh, a time to mourn and a time to dance.
—Ecclesiastes 3:4

THERE IS A BALM IN GILEAD

—An African-American spiritual

There is a balm in Gilead to make the wounded whole;

There is a balm in Gilead to heal the sin-sick soul.

Sometimes I feel discouraged,

And think my work's in vain,

But then the Holy Spirit revives my soul again.

CHAPTER THIRTEEN

THE SHEPHERD OF

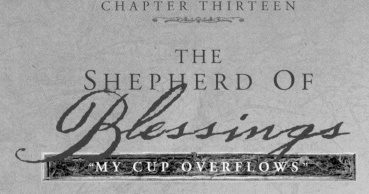

Blessings

"MY CUP OVERFLOWS"

IT'S A GOD THING

Susan is a sensitive, romantic, Southern girl with a love of anything frilly and feminine. She had always dreamed of being a wife and mother and growing old living her faith. Right on schedule, she married her childhood sweetheart Bobby and had a son they both cherished. Life couldn't get any better. It could and did get worse.

Delight yourself in the LORD and he will give you the desires of your heart.

—Psalm 37:4

At forty, instead of enjoying their empty nest years together, Susan has become Bobby's caregiver as he suffers from a slow-moving, terminal disease. He's good-natured, and it's obvious that Susan is still his princess, but she is living her faith in ways she never imagined.

Recently, Susan attended her annual church ladies' dinner. One of the women opened her spacious, beautifully decorated home and each of the thirty ladies brought a covered dish. Tables graced with a variety of tablecloths, lovely dishes, and crystal filled each room of the large downstairs.

For Susan this was a rare time out; a break from working full-time while providing care for Bobby. One of the highlights of the evening was a time of sharing about what they had learned about themselves and their walk with the Lord in the past year. Life had always been a joy for Susan, but this night, Susan was blessed in a way she never expected.

Loretta, an older woman Susan admired and hoped to emulate, praised her for her devotion to Bobby. She described Susan as a "regal queen" who wheels her husband into the sanctuary each Sunday. She was so impressed that Susan spake to Bobby with kindly respect. Loretta saw Bobby and Susan as a reflection of God's love and a wonderful example of what marriage is supposed to be—for better or worse.

Loretta's comments touched Susan because she felt the praise was undeserved. *How could I be praised,* she thought, *when I continually struggle with exhaustion, fear, guilt, and depression?* Like so many caregivers, Susan simply does what she knows her husband would do for her if she was the one who was sick. For her, the blessing of hearing she's doing an excellent job in a demanding situation was the best part of the evening.

Oscar Wilde said, "What seem to us as bitter trials are often blessings in disguise." Naturally, Susan would much prefer her husband to be healthy, but her growing faith is a blessing she wouldn't trade. That faith is encouraged by unexpected gifts in the midst of frustrations.

Last Christmas, Susan knew there wouldn't be anything under the tree from her husband, but that didn't stop her from shopping for things she knew would bring him joy. She brushed away tears of self-pity and did all she could to make sure Bobby had a special day.

Susan's boss, Jaci, is not only her supervisor but her friend. She also knows Susan is a romantic. Jaci secretly bought a present and gave it to Bobby, explaining that the gift was for him to give to Susan.

Christmas morning, Bobby with his deteriorating disease, beamed as Susan opened the beautifully wrapped package under the tree. Warm tears splashed to the tissue. She could barely see the beautiful designer purse she had long wanted but knew she couldn't afford. Even more touching for Susan was the radiant smile on Bobby's face as he watched her exult over the gift. It mattered little to Susan or Bobby that he had not chosen or purchased the purse.

The grief of caregiving for a spouse is never more pronounced than on Valentine's Day, yet even then Susan was surprised. Shortly after she got home from work a dozen red roses were delivered with a card signed, "Love, Bobby." That special boss, surely acting on a prompting from the Holy Spirit, had arranged for the flowers to reach Susan on a day when she would be feeling her lowest.

Like other caregivers, Susan is often asked how she can continue living with so much loss in her life. Susan's answer is simple: With each disappointment, she draws closer to the Shepherd, and He fills her emptiness and heals her pain.

Susan has learned what Nancy Missler spoke of when she said, "Most of us still rate the events of our lives as either a 'good' thing or a 'bad' thing, but when we're finally able to merge all the events of our lives into the category of a God thing, then we will be where He wants us."

For Susan, caregiving is a continuous series of choices, most of them coming after a string of losses that seem to tip the scale on the side of discontent. The Shepherd is well aware of choices and events and shares His blessings through individuals like Loretta and Jaci. These blessings and the Shepherd's grace help Susan be the wife and caregiver she has been called to be——one day at a time.

Be on the lookout for mercies. The more we
look for them, the more of them we will see.
Blessings brighten when we count them.
—Maltbie D. Babcock

God's gifts put
man's best dreams
to shame.
—Elizabeth Barrett
Browning

Let them give thanks to the LORD for his unfailing love
and his wonderful deeds for men, for he satisfies the
thirsty and fills the hungry with good things.
—Psalm 107:8, 9

THE DOXOLOGY

—Thomas Ken

Praise God, from whom all blessings flow;

Praise Him, all creatures here below;

Praise Him above, ye heavenly host;

Praise Father, Son, and Holy Ghost.

Amen.

CHAPTER FOURTEEN

THE
SHEPHERD WHO
Loves

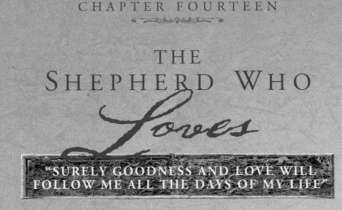

"SURELY GOODNESS AND LOVE WILL FOLLOW ME ALL THE DAYS OF MY LIFE"

THE GREATEST OF THESE

I gave a vocal concert at my husband's nursing home one Christmas. The familiar, upbeat, holiday favorites brought smiles to staff and residents. Bright decorations and tinsel hung from the artificial trees. Cutouts of Santa, his reindeer, and elves graced the walls. The nativity was conspicuously absent.

For thirty minutes, I sang a mix of secular and religious carols to the delight of everyone with the exception of one woman. Her husband sang along, but

See, I have engraved you on the palms of my hands.
—Isaiah 49:16

she stared ahead without opening her mouth—until the last song.

As the introduction played, I watched this wizened figure in a wheelchair. Her face brightened as her husband leaned close. "Silent night, holy night," I sang. By the second verse, I noticed her lips moving but with different words. I walked

closer and watched as this couple performed their own duet—he in English, she in German.

Despite the many times I had seen this woman, I had never heard her speak a word. She was obviously over ninety and had lost the ability to make conversation. I didn't know her mental capabilities, but for this one song, at least, her memory was flawless. The couple held hands as they sang, each in their native language, a song filled with eternal hope.

Caregiving is never easy and grief is a part of the good-bye process. But for those few minutes, their love made things beautiful and they embodied one face of caregiving. They reminded me of the little boy who told the story about when his grandmother got arthritis and couldn't bend over to paint her toenails anymore. When that happened, his grandfather polished each of her toes, even after his hands were bent with arthritis.

Caregivng isn't only about elderly loved ones who have lived a full life. Too often it's about a parent watching a child die long before his or her time.

Ruth is a caregiver for three of her four children. She is constantly looking for ways to show her love and share laughter. Cindy is the youngest resident of a care facility, but the other two children still live at home with Ruth.

One day her oldest daughter, Sue, went to the thrift store to buy a present for Cindy. Sue found an aquamarine, satin bridesmaid dress for the princely sum of ten dollars. When they presented it to Cindy, she was all smiles. After they helped her into the dress, they discovered the bosom was too large. Instead of admitting defeat, Ruth placed one of Cindy's plush toys in the dress. Mother and daughters laughed till they cried. And Cindy, toothless and now weighing less than ninety pounds, was a full-busted woman for  the first time in her life. Three hours later, even after watching a video, Cindy still had the toy tucked in place and was hugging another gift—a white bunny rabbit wearing a dress.

Sometimes caregiving is multi-generational. Cindy's son, Daniel, has to live with his grandma Ruth. One week Daniel's counselor suggested that Daniel go see his mother in the nursing home and talk to her about the things she did that made him angry when he was growing up; and also, to apologize for his past behavior.

Seeing his mother in the nursing home had been difficult for Daniel. As Ruth drove her grandson to the nursing home, they talked about the fact that he had only visited his mother

once before. When they arrived Daniel asked his grandmother to stay in the car, only to return fifteen minutes later. They drove home in silence.

Ruth was cooking dinner when Cindy called a few hours later. Her speech was nearly impossible to understand, but eventually Ruth deciphered Cindy's tear-filled words.

"Baby Danny came to see me. Baby Danny came to see me."

Ruth listened intently to her forty-seven-year-old baby. She had worried how Cindy must have felt when Daniel told her the things that made him feel badly growing up. Instead, all Cindy remembered about the visit was the love shown. Her baby Danny had come to visit.

Lydia Maria Child said, "The cure for all the ills and wrongs, the cares, the sorrows, and the crimes of humanity all lie in the one word love." The Shepherd is that love, that cure. A young boy was asked to describe love. He could have been talking about the elderly couple singing "Silent Night" in the nursing home or Ruth's family when he answered, "There are two kinds of love—our love and God's love. But God makes both kinds."

Treasure the love you receive above all. It will survive long after your gold and good health have vanished.
—Og Mandino

Each of you should look not only to your own interests, but also to the interests of others.
—Philippians 2:4

And now these three remain: faith, hope and love. But the greatest of these is love.
—I Corinthians 13:13

LOVE LIFTED ME

—JAMES ROWE

Love lifted me!

Love lifted me!

When nothing else could help

Love lifted me.

CHAPTER FIFTEEN

THE
SHEPHERD OF
Joy

**"AND I WILL DWELL IN THE HOUSE
OF THE LORD FOREVER"**

IN THE HEART OF THE LIVING

Betty-Anne married a man who had lost his
first wife from a genetic disease. She chose to
become a stepmother to four young boys who
had lost their mother. Some would say that
bringing children into the world, knowing they
might suffer from that same genetic disease was
foolish. But in loving this man, she took on the
possible challenge of one day being a caregiver.

*Know that the LORD
is God. It is he who
made us, and we are
his we are his people,
the sheep of his pasture.*
—Psalm 100:3

Betty-Anne thinks of her stepchildren as
gifts from God, and of course, they are. Instead of four at-
risk children, she sees four special people created in God's

image—four unique individuals allowed to enter the world for a purpose that only God can define. Even though one of the children died in a hospital and another committed suicide after his diagnosis, Betty-Anne's grief didn't destroy her love.

God walked every step with this family then, and He is still walking with them today. Betty-Anne watched as her daughter-in-law trusted God for the right words when the walls crumbled around her grandson who is currently suffering from that same genetic disease. When he could no longer manage money or make decisions, God gave Betty-Anne's daughter-in-law the wisdom for a strategic plan that would give him independence while keeping him safe. She bathes and feeds him along with fighting isolation and bed sores with vigor. Despite the fact that his struggles mean he's lost his earthly dreams and eventually, his life, Betty-Anne's grandson truly understands that the Shepherd is his best friend.

One of Betty-Anne's most joy-filled possessions is a picture of four shiny-faced boys in bathrobes and pajamas on Christmas Eve. Each time she sees that picture she thinks of a God incapable of making mistakes. A God who loves us so much that He sent His son to earth knowing Jesus would one day die on the cross for each of us, including those four shiny faces.

The moments that bring us joy might be temporary, but those memories can last forever. Sometimes the moments that help us through difficult times aren't even related to our own situation.

Betty-Anne once shared that the most heart-warming sight is the elderly couple that sits in front of her at church on Sunday each week. She's known them for years as a joyful, quiet, caring couple. Now, however, the wife has developed dementia. Each Sunday, as the hymns are sung, she and her husband look into each other's eyes. He remembers a time when she sang with joy, and as he gazes into her eyes, he sings the words she has forgotten.

We need deliberately to call to mind the joys of our journey.
—George A. Buttrick

Seeing this husband and wife brings joy to Betty-Anne, and that joy helps her as she watches her grandson journey to the end of his time on earth.

The Shepherd knows every heartache involved in caring for those we love. He is the author of every memory, memories made up of things unnoticed at the time or monumental milestones. We may not be able to live in a world without sorrow, but with the Shepherd's help, we can choose to live in joy.

Sorrow is one of the things that are lent, not given. A thing that is lent may be taken away; a thing that is given is not taken away. Joy is given; sorrow is lent.
—Amy Carmichael

You turned my wailing into dancing; you removed my sackcloth and clothed me with joy.
—Psalm 30:11

JOYFUL, JOYFUL WE ADORE THEE

—HENRY J. VAN DYKE

Joyful, joyful, we adore Thee,

God of glory, Lord of love;

Hearts unfold like flowers before Thee,

Opening to the sun above.

Melt the clouds of sin and sadness;

Drive the dark of doubt away;

Giver of immortal gladness,

Fill us with the light of day!

*"The gift of life . . . no less beautiful when it is
accompanied by illness or weakness . . . mental or
physical handicaps, loneliness or old age. Indeed,
at these times, human life gains extra splendor
as it requires our special care, concern, and reverence."*
—Cardinal Terence Cooke

Carmen Leal has experienced first-hand the Shepherd's
guidance through her caregiving journey. She is the author
of six books including *Faces of Huntington's* and *Portraits of
Huntington's.* A storyteller with a dramatic testimony, she is a
popular presenter at women's retreats, church groups, conventions, and conferences.

For more caregiving resources please visit:
http://www.thetwentythirdpsalm.com

*Thank you to those who graciously shared their caregiving
stories. Your strength and love inspires those around you.*

Great *opportunities* to help **others** seldom come, but *small ones* surround us every day.

—*Sally Koch*